So Many Ways
FAMILY

SKYE+FAM

illustrated by Noa Marie Palumbo

Dedication

From Skye's family to yours - We dedicate this book to YOU and your family!

Acknowledgments

We are thankful for our families and friends, especially:

- Sharon S. for her support of Joe and the boys, and the many conversations and research in the early days that served as the seeds that grew into this book

- Andrea Bastiani Archibald, Ph.D. (Developmental Psychologist, former Executive of Girl Scouts of the USA and Raising Awesome Girls)

- Dr. Rachel Dew (Doctor of Integrative Wellness and Self-Development Author)

- Colleen Marchi (Psychologist, Children's book author, Military spouse)

- Laura Boram (Waldorf teacher extraordinaire)

You mamas went above and beyond - not only uplifting us when we needed it most, but also helping us through the lens of your professional expertise to make this book truly holistic.

A story about celebrating the imperfectly perfect beauty of families.

Dear Readers,

Many children can start the process of individuation and begin seeing themselves outside of their parental units as early as age nine - Some younger, some older. During this time of awakening, a strong sense of self and belonging are equally needed to thrive, and it is family where most of us find these at first. Yet, it can be hard for some of us (children and adults) to stay connected, especially when we face changes or adversities in life and are bombarded with images and notions of "what" a family is or "should be."

Throughout this book, Skye serves as our little guide towards the realization that:

There is no one way (or "right" type) of person or family.

Skye believes that having healthy relationships with others begins with one's self. No matter who we are, what circumstances we are born into, where we come from or are headed - each of us possesses an internal superpower:

We can practice self-love and being kind to ourselves - just the way we are. We can accept, relate to, and build our family - from where it is. By embracing our family as imperfectly perfect, we find our special space within it, and ultimately we take our important place in this world.

This book serves as unique, one-on-one time of reading and reflecting with your children. We hope that you and the kiddos make it your own, and know that your own inner child and your children will meet somewhere in this book.

Each time you read this book, you may find yourself drawn to another part of the storyline. The sharing portion in the book's second half is equally important to the storytelling portion in the beginning. Our intention was to give you and the children precious free space to wonder, feel, go a bit deeper about yourself and your family, and connect.

As you find nuggets of good, beauty, and strength within your family's story, please share and empower others with your gift of inner peace and the powerful tools you will have to co-create healthy relationships and happy families for generations to come.

Skye's deepest wish for you with this book is that you feel proud of yourself for this inner work.

**May your bond with the family you have strengthen,
and may your relationships with those
you choose to call your family deepen!**

In service and gratitude,
Skye's Fam

Skye is nine years old.

When Skye thinks of FAMILY,
she imagines a big gathering of people that play different roles in her life.

Skye is super close to some members of her family,
and there are some she may not be as close to at this moment.

She lives with some members of her family,
and there are some she lives far away from.

But Skye says that...

"No matter what, they are all in my life story for a reason.

I accept, relate, and choose them
as my way to be family."

Skye says that her extended family is big and fun!

Right away, she thinks of three (way older) brothers, two sets of grandparents, cousins, aunts, uncles, and family friends.

Visits, calls, FaceTimes, pictures, videos, and messages keep Skye connected with her family and friends all over the country and the world.

At the same time, Skye feels that her immediate family st home is small and close.

Skye spends her days with her parents
(who she still loves calling Mommy and Daddy!)
and twenty furry siblings (chickens, dogs, cats, guinea pigs, bunny, and fish.)

At school, she loves the farm animals (llama, goose, cow, goats, pigs, and more chickens)
and the "Girl Squad" - her group of besties.

Having shared with you her one way to be family, Skye insists:

"This doesn't mean that YOU need to think of family this way."

Skye is curious:

"When you think of family, who and what do YOU think about?"

(Share out loud or simply think about it.
It's perfectly okay for it to take some time to answer, and for your reflections to change with time.)

Skye is a big girl and she has BIG questions for you...

"Like me, have YOU also wondered about... What FAMILY fully means?
Have you ever felt that different families are like
different wildflowers in a meadow?"

"Have you also noticed families different than yours?

And the many different things families can DO and BE together?"

(Share out loud or simply think about it.

It's perfectly okay for it to take some time to answer, and for your reflections to change with time.)

Some families are like ours. Other families are different than ours.

"All families are exactly the way they are meant to be
– imperfectly perfect – and full of infinite possibilities and potential."

Once upon a family...

There were a bunch of different kinds of people
who shared time and space together on Earth.

Some were human families. Others were families with humans and pets.

These families were magical because they loved themselves,
and they loved each other.

They did happy things together.

They found and created happiness together.

They were a FAMILY.

Different families do all sorts of different things together!

Skye and her family
love hanging out, cooking, traveling, meditating, and creating together.

Skye's favorite thing to do with her family is
going on long walks after dinner together.

Skye is curious:

"What are your favorite things to do with YOUR family?"

(Share out loud or simply think about it.
It's perfectly okay for it to take some time to answer, and for your reflections to change with time.)

PLAY together.

Some families play in the park together.
Other families play music together.

RIDE together.

Some families go for long drives together.

Other families ride their own wheels together.

EAT together.

Some families grill and BBQ together.
Other families cook and bake together.

BUILD together.

Some families build toy forts together.

Other families build a treehouse together.

TAKE BREAKS together.

Some families visit the aquarium together.
Other families have a zoo at home and have silly fun together.

MINDFUL together.

Some families meditate at home or connect with nature together.
Other families visit Temple, Synagogue, Church, or Mosque together.

CLEAN together.

Some families clean up the neighborhood together.
Other families clean dishes in the kitchen together.

ACTIVE together.

Some families work out in the gym or work on the farm together.
Other families jump rope in the driveway together.

GROW AND CHANGE together.

Some families welcome a new baby from the belly together.
Other families choose to grow the family from the heart together.
And other families remember a loved one they miss together.

JOIN together.

Families blend together in many ways.
Some families have bonus parents/children/siblings, and half-siblings that come together.
And other families have foster parents, grandparents, or caregivers
that hold the family together.

CREATIVE together.

Some families paint and mold clay together.
Other families make crafts together.

READ together.

Some families read braille together.
Other families read books together.

UPS AND DOWNS together.

All families go through their own ups and downs together.
Some families have more than enough together.
Other families work towards having enough together.

DO GOOD together.

Some families give their time and effort to volunteer together.
Other families gather items to donate together.

Skye knows that
we all have rough moments and tough days sometimes.

When she does,
her family makes her feel better.

Skye says that she feels safe and supported
by her family
when they help her focus on her breathing.

They take calming breaths together.

Skye is curious:

"How does YOUR family help comfort you when you have a tough day?"

(Share out loud or simply think about it.

It's perfectly okay for it to take some time to answer, and for your reflections to change with time.)

Skye is curious:

"Just as you are – without changing a thing ...

Can you find just three ways (there are so many!)

how you have helped make YOUR family the way it is today?"

(Reader guides child into a simple, positive, and judgment-free exploration of roles in the family.

Example: Are they the oldest, middle or youngest one? Are they a single child? Or a blended combination? Are they animal lovers? Or the creative one in the family? Organized one? Adventurous one? The planner? The spontaneous one? Quiet one? Entrepreneurial one?)

Now let's flip that:

"Just as they are – without changing a thing ...

Can you think about how YOUR family has helped make you, YOU?"

(Reader guides child into exploring how the family supports and encourages them with their hobbies, passions, and dreams and helps them overcome challenges.)

Skye is curious:

"Did you know that each of us and each family is so important to our planet
- individually and together -
EXACTLY AS WE ARE?"

Families are about being and growing together.

Families are about who we are and how we love
– ourselves and each other.

Some families are big, loud, and rambunctious together.

Other families are smaller and chill together.

Some families live in busy cities.

Other families live off of the land.

Families get to be unique and special together.

Some families are related by birth and by genes (not those 👖, silly!)

Other families are made by choice
like blending two families, being a surrogate, adopting, and fostering.

And other families are held by mentors, mother- and father-figures,
and friendships.

Some families live
all together.

Other families share time
across more than one
home.

Some families get to have one mom and one dad.

Other families get to have one parent,
two moms, two dads,
or important caregivers that hold the family together.

Some families get to stay put together.
Other families get to move around together.

"When we seek within,
we find gratitude for our family – just as it is.

Our family is grateful for us, too – just as we are.

Isn't it amazing that ...

There are so many ways to be family!"

Skye is curious:

"Just as you are without changing a thing...

Can you think three ways you have helped your family today?"

(Share out loud or simply think about it.

It's perfectly okay for it to take some time to answer, and for your reflections to change with time.)

Now let's flip that.

"Just as you are without changing a thing...

Can you think three ways your family has helped you today?"

(Share out loud or simply think about it.

It's perfectly okay for it to take some time to answer, and for your reflections to change with time.)

Skye is curious:

"What is one thing about your family that is SIMILAR to other families you know?

(Share out loud or simply think about it.

It's perfectly okay for it to take some time to answer, and for your reflections to change with time.)

Now let's flip that.

"What is one thing about your family that is UNIQUE or DIFFERENT

from other families you know?

(Share out loud or simply think about it.

It's perfectly okay for it to take some time to answer, and for your reflections to change with time.

Skye says...

"I am most grateful for the many happy and joyful times with my family."

She invites you to come up with what YOU are thankful for about your family.

"What do you always want to remember about your family?"

(Share just one out loud or simply think about it.

Skye encourages you to write down the rest that come to your mind on paper or draw them out on sticky notes in places you can see them often as beautiful reminders. When you see one tomorrow, feel free to say your gratitude out loud and proud!)

LET'S PRACTICE MINDFULNESS TOGETHER!

Little nightly reflections and simple daily reminders are a sweet and fun way to practice gratitude in your safe space.

Skye says that...

"Deep down, we know that being grateful is not limited to what happened (or didn't happen) to us.

We can and are able to practice feeling grateful:

FOR EVERYTHING THAT IS AND THAT ISN'T.

FOR EVERYTHING THAT MAY BE AND THAT MAY NOT BE.

FOR EVERYTHING THAT HAPPENED AND THAT DIDN'T HAPPEN
FOR US – not to us!

Each of us is born with this knowingness that we may have forgotten.

Remember, this is our inner superpower:

YOU get to remember and activate your inner superhero whenever you need it."

Skye invites you to flutter your eyes to a close for a few mindful moments.

As you start to go within,
see if you can take one (then two, then three)
big, deep, long breaths along with her.

Here we go ...

Breathe in until your belly is like a balloon.

Breathe out like you are blowing out a candle.

Breathe in. Breathe out.

Breathe in. Breathe out.

Grrrrrreat job, super-meditators!

Skye invites you to take this time to just feel how similar you and your family are to other families - without judging or changing a thing.

Breathe in until your belly is like a balloon.
Breathe out like you are blowing out a candle.
Breathe in. Breathe out.
Breathe in. Breathe out.

Skye feels that when we look inward, we are one. We are related by love.

Breathe in until your belly is like a balloon.
Breathe out like you are blowing out a candle.
Breathe in. Breathe out.
Breathe in. Breathe out.

When you are ready to flutter your eyes open, Skye invites you to look around you.

When we open our eyes and look outside ourselves and our family,
we feel how unique we are, how unique our family is from others.

Skye feels that when we look outward, we are each unique and special.

Can you be both - be one with others and be unique? Yes!

You are like others AND you are different from others too. Isn't that amazing?

"Aren't we all the same in oh so many different ways?"

Now, let's activate another superpower you have - your imagination!

As you drift off into your imagination,
Skye invites you to say to yourself along with her:

"I love myself. I do.

I love the family I get to have. I do.

I love to do happy things together. I do.

I love to be happy together. I do.

I love the family I get to make. I do.

I love us. I do."

Here is the most important thing that Skye wants to share with you ...

"We are not just born into families.
We pick and find them.
We also make them.
We are family.

Families come in all shapes, sizes, and colors.

Just like the many wildflowers in a single meadow,
there are so many ways to be family!"

One last time (until next time)...

Skye is curious:

"Have you looked at your family through her eyes before?"

YOU can be curious too!

Each of us eventually gets to make our own family - of one or of many.

Each of us eventually gets to choose to have pets or maybe not.

Each of us gets to choose who we want to be and how we want to relate.

You are important. You matter.

Your family is important. Your family matters.

You are amazing and brave - without exception.

You get to have a family. You get to make a family.

Your family can certainly influence you and help you,
but your family does not make you nor break you.

"You make you. You make family."

BONUS WORKBOOK

FREE SPACE TP DOODLE AND JOURNAL

Think about you and your family doing something fun together,
and try to either draw (or find and paste) a fun picture of you with your family.

Feel free to also write down a few short, positive words that come to your mind
when you think of your family.
(Some ideas: Silly, Happy, Strong, Fun, Busy, Awesome, Hard working, Best, Love, Home, etc.)

What is your favorite family tradition or an awesome activity that your family does together?

Feel free to draw it out or paste a fun picture or write words about it.

(Some ideas: Games, holidays, foods, etc. that you enjoy with your family?)

What are some of your happiest moments or memories with your family?

Feel free to write them down or draw them out.
(Some ideas: Fun trips, adventures, family hobbies, etc.)

I am grateful for my family because we/they ...

1.

2.

3.

My family is grateful for me because I ...

1.

2.

3.

Collect some family pictures and mementos like train tickets and postcards and add them below to create your 'So Many Ways To Be MY Family' scrapbook as a family project over the weekend or on your next break!

Collect some family pictures and mementos like train tickets and postcards and add them below to create your 'So Many Ways To Be MY Family' scrapbook as a family project over the weekend or on your next break!

Collect some family pictures and mementos like train tickets and postcards and add them below to create your 'So Many Ways To Be MY Family' scrapbook as a family project over the weekend or on your next break!

Collect some family pictures and mementos like train tickets and postcards and add them below to create your 'So Many Ways To Be MY Family' scrapbook as a family project over the weekend or on your next break!

ABOUT THE AUTHOR

So Many Ways To Be Family is co-authored by a family: Skye, Joe, and Payel Farasat.

Skye, age nine, co-authored her first book So Many Ways To Be Family with her family. Skye serves as a little guide throughout the book which shares a diverse and inclusive narrative that there is not just one type of perfect family. Skye has been meditating with her parents since she was a baby. She shares her simple yet powerful technique of staying mindful and grounded while forming her space in the family and finding her place in the world. Skye is a fourth grader and has been a student of Waldorf education since age four. Since Waldorf pedagogy centers around inner work, Skye leaves us with exploratory questions and white space for interactive exercises, so we too can practice our inner work around our own family along with her.

Joe and Payel are Skye's dad and mom. Both are financial services executives, certified in coaching, consulting, and mindfulness. Joe envisioned the concept of the book after his divorce many years ago when he searched everywhere for a comforting and empowering children's book for his three young sons that was supportive of blended families. After getting married and growing their family, Joe and Payel expanded the concept to include cultural, socioeconomic, and mixed families. Skye couldn't agree more and so, they started working on completing the book together during the lockdown when Skye was age seven and displaying her own resonation with mindfulness, inner work, and storytelling.

ABOUT THE ILLUSTRATOR

So Many Ways To Be Family is illustrated by Noa Marie Palumbo.

Noa and Skye met at school back in 2019 when Noa, a graduating twelfth grader then, walked Skye around the campus on her first day of first grade.

Noa's artwork is Waldorf inspired and the medium is chalk pastels.

ABOUT THE BOOK

It is family at first where most of us find our self-esteem and sense of belonging. However, we start seeing ourselves outside of our parents and family pretty early on in childhood - with many starting to individuate around age nine. During the ups and downs of life, books like So Many Ways To Be Family strive to make it easier for children (and adults) to hold on to our self-love and sense of belonging - especially as we get bombarded with images and notions of "what" a family is or "should be."

So Many Ways To Be Family seeds a simple, impactful practice of self-love surrounded by a celebration of families and all the varieties we come in - whether it be big or small, look alike or different, have a single parent or two!

Skye serves as a little guide towards the realization that there is no one way (or "right" type) of person or family. She gently takes the beautiful path towards accepting and embracing family - exactly as it is - imperfectly perfect. Skye reminds us that by staying consciously and habitually aware of our personal big picture, we can more easily deepen our sense of self, find our special space within our family, navigate relationships, and ultimately take our important place in this world.